PENGUIN BOOKS

THE WASTE LAND

Martin Rowson has been a freelance cartoonist since leaving university in 1982. His work has appeared in the *New Statesman, Guardian, Independent, Today* and *Sunday Correspondent,* where he draws a weekly cartoon strip on the book pages. His two previous books are *Scenes from the Lives of the Great Socialists* and *Lower than Vermin: An Anatomy of Thatcher's Britain.*

Martin Rows   ied w
in south

THE WASTE LAND

Martin Rowson

PENGUIN BOOKS

PENGUIN BOOKS

Published by the Penguin Group
Penguin Books Ltd, 27 Wrights Lane, London w8 5tz, England
Viking Penguin, a division of Penguin Books USA Inc.
375 Hudson Street, New York, New York 10014, USA
Penguin Books Australia Ltd, Ringwood, Victoria, Australia
Penguin Books Canada Ltd, 2801 John Street, Markham, Ontario, Canada l3r 1b4
Penguin Books (NZ) Ltd, 182–190 Wairau Road, Auckland 10, New Zealand

Penguin Books Ltd, Registered Offices: Harmondsworth, Middlesex, England

First published in the USA by Harper & Row, Publishers, New York 1990
Published in Penguin Books with revised notes 1990
1 3 5 7 9 10 8 6 4 2

Printed in England by Clays Ltd, St Ives plc

For ANNA *(il miglior fabbro)*
FRED
and JOHN STEANE, *with whom
I first walked down these mean
streets...........*

With thanks to........
Anna Clarke, Shaun Whiteside, Robert Buttimore, Jon Lewin, Roy Castle, Ian Thomson, Dave Eva, Peter Illsley, Dr. & Mrs. K.E.K. Rowson, Bill Ogden, Charlie Adley, Mary-Lou Legg and Caradoc King

Then there is the pale, pale blonde with anæmia of some non-fatal but incurable type. She is very languid and very shadowy and she speaks softly out of nowhere and you can't lay a finger on her because in the first place you don't want to and in the second place she is reading THE WASTE LAND or Dante in the original, or Kafka or Kierkegaard or studying Provençal......

Raymond Chandler, THE LONG GOODBYE

"May I ask Mr. Marlowe a question?"
"Certainly, Amos."
He put down the overnight case inside the door and she went in past me and left us.
"'I grow old... I grow old... I shall wear the bottoms of my trousers rolled.' What does that mean, Mr. Marlowe?"
"Not a bloody thing. It just sounds good."
He smiled. "That is from the Love Song of J. Alfred Prufrock. Here's another one. 'In the room the women come and go Talking of Michelangelo.' Does that suggest anything to you, sir?"
"Yeah — it suggests to me that the guy didn't know very much about women."
"My sentiments exactly, sir. Nonetheless I admire T. S. Eliot very much."
"Did you say 'nonetheless'?"

Raymond Chandler, THE LONG GOODBYE

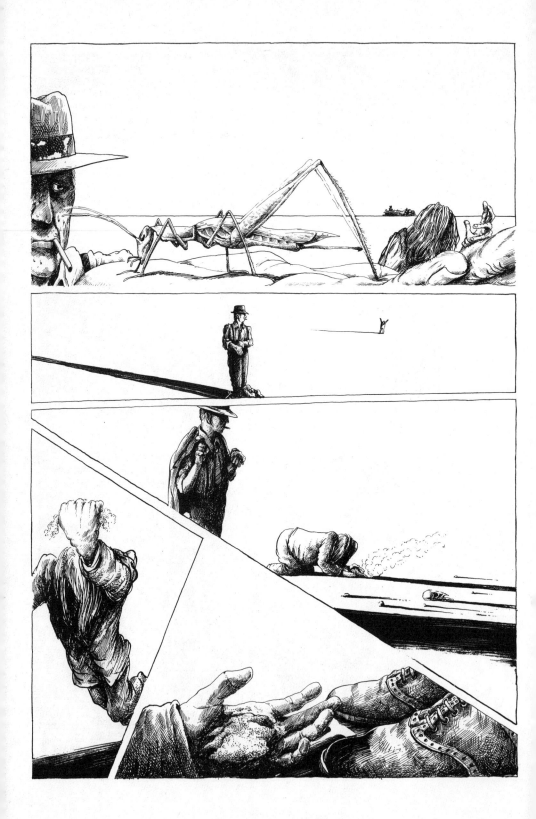

SO WE WALKED AND *HE* TALKED AND DANCED AND WHEN HE DECIDED TO *ROLL OVER* AND *PLAY DEAD*, IT WAS TIME FOR ME TO WALK AWAY...

FRISCH WEHT DER WIND DER HEIMAT ZU, HERR MARLOWE, MEIN IRISCH KIND, WO WEILEST DU?

BUT THAT WAS *THEN*. NOW, MILES WASN'T *PLAYING* DEAD ANYMORE. THE COUNTESS WAS STILL HITTING ME WITH THE *KRAUTSPIEL*....

SHE GAVE ME *TEN BUCKS* TO FIND WHATEVER IT WAS SHE *SOUGHT*. IT WASN'T CLEAR. WAS IT THE *SLED*, THE *ARCHDUKE* OR THIS *IRISH KID?* SHE'D GIVEN ME NOTHING TO GO ON, BUT THERE WAS NOTHING *NEW* IN *THAT*. I DECIDED TO *WALK* THE STREETS AND GET *WET*...

WHY, HELLO THERE!

AT LEAST I'D BEEN GIVEN A *NAME*. SOME *GREEK DAME* DOWNTOWN HAD A LINE IN *SEEING THE FUTURE*, WHICH WAS USE-FUL IN A CASE LIKE THIS, EVEN IF THE ONLY FUTURE I WAS INTEREST-ED IN WAS *LIQUID*, GOLDEN WITH A *MEAN MESSAGE* FOR MARLOWE IN THE TAIL. THE LAST THING I NEEDED WAS A *CRAZY KID* WITH A *BAD MEMORY* FOR FACES....

WHERE'S DA BUNCHA FLOWERS YA PROMISED, YA *BUM!!* DAT WUZ A YEAR BACK AN' I WAN' *ARMFULS!!!*

OD' UND LEER DAS MEER!

PRUFROCK GALLERY

SEEMS LIKE TODAY WAS BERLITZ LANGUAGE SCHOOL DAY...

CLOSE

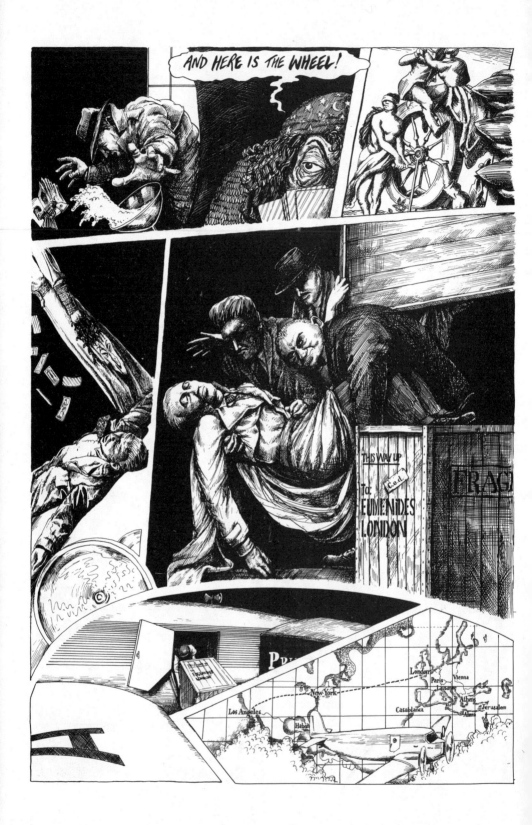

THE BAR'S *CLIENTELE* LOOKED ABOUT AS *WELCOMING* AS A BAY CITY STATION COP WHO'S JUST FOUND OUT BOTH YOUR LEGS ARE *ALREADY BROKEN*...

SO ANYWAYS, I TOLD 'ER, I DID...

GIMME A BOURBON ON THE ROCKS!

ICE? IN THIS 'EAT? YOU MUST BE BARMY!

LAWKS STREWTH LUMME LAWD LUVADUCK!

AMAZING TALES — THE BLOB FROM MARS THAT ATE BLOOMSBURY

THE *BARMAN* LOOKED LIKE YOUR *FRIENDLY LOCAL MOBSTER* WHO MAKES A *POINT* OF TELLING YOU HE DOESN'T *MINCE HIS WORDS* WHILE HE'S *MINCING YOUR FACE.* IT WAS REASSURING TO KNOW I STILL WASN'T WINNING ANY SOCIETY PAGE POLLS FOR "MOST DESIRED DETECTIVE TO GET STINKING DRUNK WITH"...

I THOUGHT IT *SMART* TO SIT STILL IN A *DARK CORNER.* NEXT TO ME TWO OLD FRAILS WERE AUDITIONING FOR WALK-ON PARTS IN "MY FAIR LADY"... BUT THE HELL WITH *THEM*...

DRINK UP PLEASE GENTS

GORBLIMEY STONE THE BLEEDIN' CROWS!

I WAS PLANNING TO GET MY *TEETH* IN FRONT OF A *DEAL OF LIQUOR*...

CHAPTER 3

SPLOSH!

GLUG GLUG GLUG

THE GUNSEL TOLD ME HIS BOSS, MR EUMENIDES, WOULD LIKE TO SEE ME. I SAID *I'D* LIKE TO SEE *HIM*. THINGS WERE GETTING TO BE SO *UNREAL* I RECKONED IT'D BE *SMART* TO PLAY THIS ONE *POLITE*...

AH, MR MARLOWE! A PLEASURE, SIR! INDEED! COME IN, SIR, DO COME IN!

HAVE A *CURRANT*, SIR. TAKE *SEVERAL*! I LIKE A MAN WHO LIKES TO EAT, SIR, INDEED I DO...

NOW, SIR, LET US TALK ABOUT THE *CUP*. BUT FIRST, SIR, ANSWER ME A QUESTION PLEASE, SO THAT WE MAY UNDERSTAND EACH OTHER FROM THE BEGINNING. ARE YOU HERE AS MR SWEENEY'S AGENT?

MAYBE I AM... IT DEPENDS...

DEPENDS ON WHAT? ON YOUR PARTNER'S WIDOW? ON MADAME SESOSTRIS, IDAHO EZ AND THE MINOAN, EH?

YOU COULD PUT IT THAT WAY...

EXCEPT, SIR, I'LL WAGER THAT NOT ONE OF THEM KNOWS EXACTLY WHAT THE *CUP* IS. NO ONE IN THIS WHOLE WIDE SWEET WORLD KNOWS EXCEPT ME.

SWELL. SO WHAT IS IT?

I'LL *AMAZE* YOU, SIR. I'LL *ASTOUND* YOU!

WHAT WOULD YOU SAY, SIR, IF I WERE TO TELL YOU THAT THE CUP IS *REALLY* AND *TRULY* THE *HOLY GRAIL* ITSELF? THERE, SIR, WHAT D'YOU SAY TO THAT?

EUMENIDES' "SMYRNA GOLD" CURRANTS

THE RIVER WAS ABOUT AS CLEAN AS *CITY HALL*. IT MADE ME FEEL KIND OF *HOMESICK*. IT MADE ME FEEL LIKE *HANGING UP* MY *OAT*, MARRYING A *FISH WIFE*, SETTING UP A LITTLE HOME IN THE *GUTTER* AND THINKING ABOUT *SETTLING DOWN....*

AND IF I HAD A PET SEWER RAT, I'D CALL HIM *GEORGE...*

THE BOAT DRIFTED DOWNSTREAM WITH THE *TURNING TIDE*. I'D SEEN CLEANER THINGS THAN THIS RIVER COMING OUT OF *DOGS*. I THOUGHT ABOUT WHAT *PROGRESS* I'D MADE ON THE *LARISCH CASE*... THINGS WERE MOVING ABOUT AS *FAST* AS THE *OIL SLICK* WE WERE *BOBBING* AROUND ON. AND AS FOR GETTING TO THE *BOTTOM* OF THE *MILES BUSINESS*...

SO FAR I'D *BARGED* IN ON SOME *CORPSES*, THE KIND OF *YOUNG LOVE* THEY BUILD CLINICS TO DEAL WITH, AN OLD TIN COCKTAIL GLASS AND A *WHOLE HEAP* OF *HOOEY*. ALL OF WHICH ADDED UP TO *PRECISELY* NOTHING...

I WAS BEGINNING TO GET THE *DISTINCT IMPRESSION* THAT I WAS *ALL WASHED UP*....

WEIA! WAGA! WAGALAWEIA! WEIALA WEIA!

NOTHING WAS CONNECTING... EXCEPT MAYBE... I REMEMBERED THE *SCRAP OF PAPER* I'D FOUND AT THE *PORTER DAME'S* PLACE...

Carthage Novelties Inc.

44310 Fisherman's Canyon, Carthage, Los Angeles County, Calif., U.S.A.

Jerusalem · Athens · Alexandria · Vienna · London

DIRECTORS: Miles & Sybil Fisher · A.N. Sweeney · Madame Sesostris · Michael T. Minoan.

AND THERE IT ALL WAS. A CRIPPLED WINO WITH BAD EYE-SIGHT AND THE *SHORT-TERM MEMORY* OF A *PRESSED CRAB SANDWICH* COULD'VE WORKED IT OUT, BUT NOT ME. THEY WERE ALL IN IT TOGETHER. SESOSTRIS, SWEENEY, THE MINOAN. YEAH. AND MILES. I'D BEEN DOPED, DUMPED, ALMOST DROWNED, BUT WORST OF ALL I'D BEEN PLAYED FOR A *SUCKER* BY MY OWN PARTNER...

L.A., L.A., THAT'S WHERE I SHOULD'VE BEEN ALL ALONG, NOT SWAPPING SOB STORIES WITH THE *SOAK SISTERS* IN SOME ZERO BURG CALLED MARGATE. I HAD TO GET BACK HOME ...

KISS ME KWIK

TO CARTHAGE THEN I CAME

CARTHAGE NOVELTIES INC KEEP OUT

CHAPTER 5:
WHAT THE THUNDER SAID

DOESN'T LOOK THE WAY YOU'D HANDLE IT, CHRIS

ME? I DIDN'T DO THIS

WELL...

LOOK AT IT THIS WAY. WE KNOW FROM HIS I.D. THAT THIS MINOAN GUY WORKED, APPARENTLY AS A *CHAUFFEUR*, FOR A DOWN-TOWN SIDE SHOW ARTIST CALLED SESOSTRIS. NOW IF SHE MAKES A LIVING *SPOOKING SUCKERS*, THAT'S HER BUSINESS. WHAT'S *OUR* BUSINESS IS THAT SHE SAYS A *PRIVATE PARTY* SHE WAS THROWING ABOUT A MONTH BACK WAS BUSTED UP BY A *GUMSHOE* WHOSE DESCRIPTION MATCHES YOUR OWN. YOU FOLLOWING ME?

THEN WE HEAR FROM *LONDON* THAT THIS SAME SESOSTRIS' *BUTLER* IS FOUND MURDERED IN A *CATHOUSE*. SOMEBODY SAYS THEY SEE AN *AMERICAN SHAMUS* WHO SOUNDS *KINDA FAMILIAR* LEAVING THE PLACE AT A TIME CORRESPONDING TO THE *KILLING*. THEN THE BRITISH POLICE SAY THEY GET *COMPLAINTS* FROM AN *ALL GIRL SINGING TROUPE* ABOUT THIS SAME SHAMUS, OR AT LEAST ONE *REMARKABLY SIMILAR*, ASKING QUESTIONS ABOUT, YOU GUESSED IT, THIS *SAME PHLEBAS.*

SHALL I GO ON? OKAY, SO *ALSO MIKE* AND HIS EMPLOYER ARE INVOLVED IN A *SHADY ENTERPRISE* OPERATING BEHIND THE NAME OF *CARTHAGE NOVELTIES*. ALSO INVOLVED, AMONG OTHERS, IS THE *DEAD PARTNER* OF A CERTAIN *DETECTIVE*. THEN, MYSTERIOUSLY, THE *WAREHOUSE* OF SAID ENTERPRISE BURSTS INTO FLAMES. AT WHICH POINT *YOU* TURN UP OUT OF THE *BLUE.* CO-INCIDENCE, HUH?

RUMBRR-R-RRRUMMMMMM
OKAY, LADY. YOU GOT YA GOODS. NOW WHAT ABOUT MA MOOLAH?
REALLY, OFFICER BURBANK! DO YOU HONESTLY EXPECT ME TO PAY YOU AFTER YOU KILLED MY HUSBAND?
WHAT? BURBANK KILLED MILES?
HEY, C'MON! SHE TOLD ME TO! MARLOWE? HEY, LET'S FACE IT, THE BABE'S BATS!
MARLOWE?
KERFHARGHZZSSFPHZZSSSZDRNENK!!!
SCREEEEEEEEEEEE
MENS' ROOM
MARLOWE!!
OOOOOOW!
Red Rock Casino
PHSSSZZTT!!

THE NOTES

SNIP SNIP SNIP SNIP

SNIP SNIP SNIP SNIP

HEY, BUB!

MY NAME'S MARLOWE. I'M A P.I. AND I'M SICK TO MY BELLY! I WANT TO KNOW WHAT THE HELL'S BEEN GOING ON! AND I WANT TO KNOW NOW!

WE'LL START WITH THE SOSOSTRIS DAME. HOW DOES SHE FIT INTO ALL OF THIS?

IAMQUE OPUS EXEGI, QUOD NEC IOVIS IRA, NEC IGNIS, NEC POTERIT FERRUM, NEC EDAX ABOLERE VETUSTAS.

BIG DEAL! SO TELL ME ABOUT THE DEAD CHAUFFEUR. HOW'S HE FIGURE? AND WHAT'S THE BIG BEEF ABOUT LONDON AND THE GODDAM RIVER? AND EUGENIDES, AND THE KID WITH THE HYACINTHS... HOW'S ALL THAT HANG TOGETHER, HUH?

LE POÈTE EST SEMBLABLE AU PRINCE DES NUÉES QUI HANTE LA TEMPÊTE ET SE RIT DE L'ARCHER...

QUIT STALLIN', BUSTER! SPILL THE BEANS OR I'LL WASTE YOU, SO HELP ME!

HEY, GUMSHOE!

IDAHO!

SACRÉ BLEU! AVEZ-VOUS LA PLUME DE MA TANTE?

D'YA THINK A DUMB SHAMUS LIKE YOU COULDA FIGURED IT ALL OUT?

YOU BUM! SO YOU STITCHED ALL THIS UP! YOU PUT THE DAME UP TO THE WHOLE DAMN THING! THE DAME'S THE KEY, RIGHT?

PROCUL HINC, PROCUL ESTE, SEVERAE! ALL THE WOMEN ARE ONE WOMAN.

SO DAMES ARE ALL THE SAME? IS THAT ALL YOU GOT TO TELL ME?

ET ME FECERE POETAM PIERIDES, SUNT ET MIHI CARMINA. ME QUOQUE DICUNT VATEM PASTORES: SED NON EGO CREDULUS ILLIS. NAM NEQUE ADHUC VARIO VIDEOR NEC DICERE CINNA DIGNA, SED ARGUTOS INTER STREPERE ANSER OLORES.....

QUIT THE WISEGUY STUFF! GIVE ME THE JUICE ON THE GRAIL DINGIT!

IT SHOULD BE SEEN IN THE CONTEXT OF VEGETATION MYTHS...

BLAST

years 1910 to 1940

Curse abysmal inexcusable obnubilation by smart-arse emigre FELLOW TRAVELLERS of italian tough-guys.

BLAST!

the mean-minded metaphysics of CAT-FANCYING (PRUDERY-Calls to Order- Moody Silences)

BLAST

VEGETATION MYTHS? THE ONLY VEGETATION MYTH I EVER HEARD OF WAS THAT YOU CAN SIT ON YOUR ASS BEHIND A DESK IN THE D.A.'S OFFICE FOR TWENTY YEARS AND CALL IT WORK...

That's all, Folks!

THANTH THANTH THANTH, THUCKERS!!

QUOTATIONS FOR CATS

THE NOTES

Not only the title but the layout and a good deal of the incidental imagery of the book were suggested by Mr T. S. Eliot's poem *The Waste Land* (Faber & Faber). Indeed, so heavily am I indebted, Mr Eliot's poem will illuminate the complexities of the book much better than my notes can; and I recommend it (apart from the intrinsic interest of the poem itself) to anyone who thinks such illumination worth the trouble. To two cinematic works I am indebted in general, both of which have influenced our generation considerably; I mean *The Big Sleep* and *The Maltese Falcon*. Anyone who is familiar with these works will immediately recognize in the book certain references to Californian private investigators.

The references are listed by chapter and frame number.

PROLOGUE

Frame 2: Varus quoted by Servius in his note to Virgil, *Eclogues*, vi, 42.

I. THE BURIAL OF THE DEAD

Frame 2. For "dried Tuba", read "dried tuber" throughout.

17. *v.* Julian Sykes Wolsey's 1935 poem "On a Bus with J. Alfred Prufrock":

> *In the room the women came and went*
> *Talking of Vermeer of Ghent.*
> *In the room the women take a hike*
> *Talking of Jan van Eyck.*
> *In the room the women catch a bus*
> *Talking of Walter Gropius.*
> *In the room the women catch a train*
> *Talking of Michelangelo again.*

Also of interest is the minimalist poet D. N. Eva's

> *I knew a man called T. S. Eliot*
> *Who wanted to write "The Waist Land" but couldn't spelliot.*

32. St Mary Woolnoth is a City church designed by Nicholas Hawksmoor, the subject of a novel by Peter Ackroyd, author of *T. S. Eliot* (1984).

II. A GAME OF CHESS

Frames 25 & 26. For further details on the musical notation used here, cf. page 130 of *American Folk Songs* (Penguin, 1964). See also A. L. Morton's *The English Utopia* (East Berlin: Seven Seas Books) and Helen Killane's *The Songs of Burl Ives: Jarring Notes Towards a Definition of the American Male* (Mucho Macho Press).

36. One is reminded here of W. H. Auden's memorable near-palindrome: "T. Eliot, top bard, notes putrid tang emanating, is sad: I'd assign it a name, gnat dirt upset on drab pot toilet."

37. Curiously enough, Millais' "Sir Isumbras at the Ford" was Tenniel's model for the White Knight in *Through the Looking Glass*.

III. THE FIRE SERMON

Frames 11–26. I forget which of Eliot's poems these characters originally appear in, but I think one of the early ones.
   Cf. *Special Issue Small Arms of World War Two*, ed. Roy Castle (War Action Library, 1981).

26. Peggy Guggenheim's dog, "Sir Herbert Reed", is buried in her garden in Venice. See also the mosaic at the top of the staircase outside the National Gallery shop.
   Cf. Isaac Guillespie's "Eliot with an Angelus, Pound with a Fasces" from *Waiting at the Archduke's* (1934):

> Dada wouldn't buy me a Bauhaus
> Dada wouldn't buy me a Bauhaus
> Vortecism and De Stijl
> Only make me feel quite ill
> And I'd rather have a Bau bau Haus (my translation).

33. "The Chalice from the Palace". Cf. *The Court Jester*, starring Danny Kaye. The Holy Grail should not be confused with Mrs Llewellyn Lockridge Grayle in *Farewell My Lovely*.

59. Peter Ackroyd is the author of a biography of T. S. Eliot

65. "He said he was a friend of Wrinkled Doug's." Although a mere pun and not indeed a "joke", this is yet the most important gag in the book, uniting all the rest. Reflecting on the whole section, we might do well to temper Petronius's

> Foeda est in coitu et brevis voluptas
> Et taedat Veneris statim peractae

with Voltaire's highly significant comment:

> Il est plaisant qu'on fait une vertu du vice de chasteté; et voilà encore une drôle de chasteté que celle qui mène tout droit les hommes au péché d'Onan, est les filles aux pâles couleurs!

and of equally great anthropological interest is this passage from Empson's inaugural lecture as Professor of English at Sheffield:

> I was rather pleased one year in China when I had a course on modern poetry, *The Waste Land* and all that, and at the end a student wrote in a most friendly way to explain why he wasn't taking the exam. It wasn't that he couldn't understand *The Waste Land*, he said, in fact after my lectures the poem was perfectly clear: but it had turned out to be disgusting nonsense, and he had decided to join the engineering department. Now there a teacher is bound to feel solid satisfaction; he is getting definite results.

80. "Abie the Fishman". The true identity, in the Marx Brothers' film *Animal Crackers*, of the émigré Czech financier Roscoe W. Chandler. The narrative of the film involves the theft of a priceless work of art.

98. Carthage, California. Not to be confused with Carthage, Montana, or Carthage, Texas.

IV. DEATH BY WATER

During the filming of *The Big Sleep*, Bogart asked the director of the picture the significance of the dead chauffeur in the Packard dredged out of the ocean. Not knowing the answer, the director asked the scriptwriters. Equally in the dark, they phoned Chandler, who'd forgotten.

V. WHAT THE THUNDER SAID

In the first part of Chapter 5 three themes are employed: the journey from *The Treasure of the Sierra Madre*, the sound effects at the beginning of *Finnegans Wake* and images from the Tex Avery classic *What's Buzzin', Buzzard*.

Frames 1–10. The absence here of a previously dominant figure in the Eliot version is significant, and indicative of how far we've come. Cf. Nietzsche, *Die Fröhliche Wissenschaft:*

> Gott ist tot; aber so wie die Art der Menschen ist, wird es vielleicht noch jahrtausendlang Höhlen geben, in denen man seinen Schatten zeigt ... Der christliche Entschluss, die Welt hässlich und schlecht zu finden, hat die Welt hässlich und schlecht gemacht.

Cf. McLuhan, *Understanding Media*. Also, Bakunin:

если Бог сушествует, то мы бы должны были Его уничтожить

14. In fact, rather than being a *Turdus aonalaschkae pallasii*, the bird shown here is a *Turdus philomelos*. One presumes that Eliot could equally well have employed the symbolism of, say, a rock hopper penguin at this point. Cf. Kevin Killane, *The Bestiary: Zoos, Zoo Animals and the Weltschmertz* (Pathfinder, 1982).

20. "I am half sick of shadows, said the Lady of Shallot" by John Waterhouse.

29. *v*. Tennyson, *Maud*.

47. The goat here is probably a misreading of "boat". *v*. Thomas of Celano:

> *Inter oves locum praesta*
> *Et ab haedis me sequestra*
> *Statuens in parte dextra.*

49. Cf. *Inferno*, xxvi, 118.

50. Cf. Ovid, *Tristia*, III, xii, 47.

52. *v*. *El Desdichado* by Gerard de Nerval. De Nerval kept a pet lobster which he would take for walks on a leash in the Bois de Boulogne. When asked why, he replied: "It does not bark, and knows the secrets of the sea."

54. *v*. the drinking song from Fletcher's and Jonson's *The Bloody Brother*, II, ii.

55. Cf. Kyd, *The Spanish Tragedy*, additions xii, 1.71.

THE NOTES

Frame 4. Cf. *Metamorphoses*, XV, 871.

5. Cf. Baudelaire, *Les Fleurs du mal*, ii, "L'Albatros".

9. Cf. Ovid, *Amores*, II, i, 3.

10. Cf. Virgil, *Eclogues*, ix, 32.

CAST

Themselves
Chris Marlowe
Miles Fisher *his partner*
Burbank & Bleistein *Bay City Vice Squad Officers*
Countess Marie Larisch
The Hyacinth Kid
Bernie Ohls *DA's Department Investigator*
Madame Sesostris *a clairvoyante*
Sweeney *her butler*

Sybil Fisher Mary Astor
Gunsel/Young Man Carbuncular Elisha Cook Jnr.
Mr Eumenides, the Smyrna Merchant Sydney Greenstreet

The Water Babes
Dorothy Comingore, Lauren Bacall, Marlene Dietrich

Tiresias/Woman in Art Gallery Dame Edith Sitwell
Janitor/Idaho Ez
Man in Museum/Buddhist Ezra Pound
Taxi Driver Peter Ackroyd
1st Barman Craig Raine
2nd Barman Ernest Hemingway

Barflies in 1st Pub
Richard Aldington, William Carlos Williams, Henri Gaudier Brezska,
John Quinn, W. B. Yeats, Joseph Conrad, Wyndham Lewis,
Vivienne Eliot, Louis Zukofsky and T. S. Eliot

Piano player Ford Madox Ford
Mandolin player W. B. Yeats

Barflies in 2nd pub
Gertrude Stein, Edmund Wilson, Alice B. Toklas, Robert Graves,
Robert Frost, Herman Melville and Norman Mailer

Daytrippers on Boat
Richard Wagner, Aldous Huxley, Henry James,
Lord Robert Dudley, Earl of Leicester, Dante Alighieri, Elizabeth I,
William Shakespeare, Edmund Spenser, Joseph Conrad and
William Carlos Williams

Countess Larisch's houseboy Mendy Menendez

8.17.93 3.95 E. Hamilton 54681